SUPER SCIENCE

PLANTS

WRITTEN BY

Valerie Harvey

KidHaven PUBLISHING

Published in 2027 by
KidHaven Publishing, an Imprint of Greenhaven Publishing, LLC
2544 Clinton St., Buffalo, NY 14224

Written by: Valerie Harvey
Edited by: Nicola Chave
Designed by: Lucy Otter

Cataloging-in-Publication Data
Names: Harvey, Valerie.
Title: Plants / Valerie Harvey.
Description: Buffalo, NY : KidHaven Publishing, 2027. | Series: Super science | Includes glossary and index.
Identifiers: ISBN 9781534570467 (pbk.) | ISBN 9781534570474 (library bound) | ISBN 9781534570481 (ebook)
Subjects: LCSH: Plants--Juvenile literature.
Classification: LCC QK49.H378 2027 | DDC 580--dc23

Printed in China

CPSIA compliance information: Batch #QS27KH: For further information contact Greenhaven Publishing LLC at 1-844-317-7404.

Please visit our website, www.greenhavenpublishing.com.
For a free color catalog of all our high-quality books, call toll free 1-844-317-7404 or fax 1-844-317-7405.

Find us on

Image Credits. All images courtesy of Shutterstock.com, unless otherwise stated.
Cover - Dragon Images. Recurring - Leremy, Dedraw Studio. 4-5 - Gorodenkoff. 6-7 - Andriana Syvanych, Narmeria. 8-9 - Ethan Daniels, Lecia Michelle, Nigma Photography, Miriam Newitt, vetre. 10-11 - Buch and Bee. 12-13 - MVolodymyr, Nature's clicks, Wirestock Creators, Yonkou Red. 14-15 - Mandy787, Mmar Palenzuela, Nitr. 16-17 - TAMER YILMAZ, happycreator, Nicholas J Klein. 18-19 - sujesh, Heidi Danslamontagne. 20-21 - Andrew Mayovskyy, Melinda Nagy, Oleg Kovtun Hydrobio.

CONTENTS

Words that look like <u>this</u> can be found in the glossary on page 24.

SUPER START!

Science means learning about the world by watching, taking notes, and asking questions. Science helps us understand why things happen and how the world works. It's super important!

Meet our plant expert, Captain Curious! He'll lead us on a journey through gardens, forests, and fields. Are you ready to learn how plants grow, make food, and help our planet?

PERFECT PLANTS

Plants are amazing living things. They come in many different shapes, sizes, and colors. Some are tiny and some are tall.

Plants have some amazing superpowers that help us live, grow, and stay healthy. They take in the gases we don't need when we breathe out and give us fresh air to breathe in.

SEEDS

Plants start their lives as seeds. Seeds come from adult plants and get spread around. Seeds are spread in different ways.

SOME SEEDS ARE BLOWN AWAY BY THE WIND.

SOME SEEDS FALL INTO WATER AND GET CARRIED AWAY.

SOME SEEDS ARE SPREAD BY ANIMALS. THESE SEEDS MIGHT STICK TO THE ANIMALS OR GET EATEN BY THEM.

SOME SEED PODS BURST OPEN AND LAUNCH THEIR SEEDS.

The different ways plants spread their seeds is an amazing superpower!

HOW PLANTS GROW

Plants need several things to grow. First, seeds need the right kind of soil and water. Then they will germinate. When a seed germinates, it grows roots and a shoot.

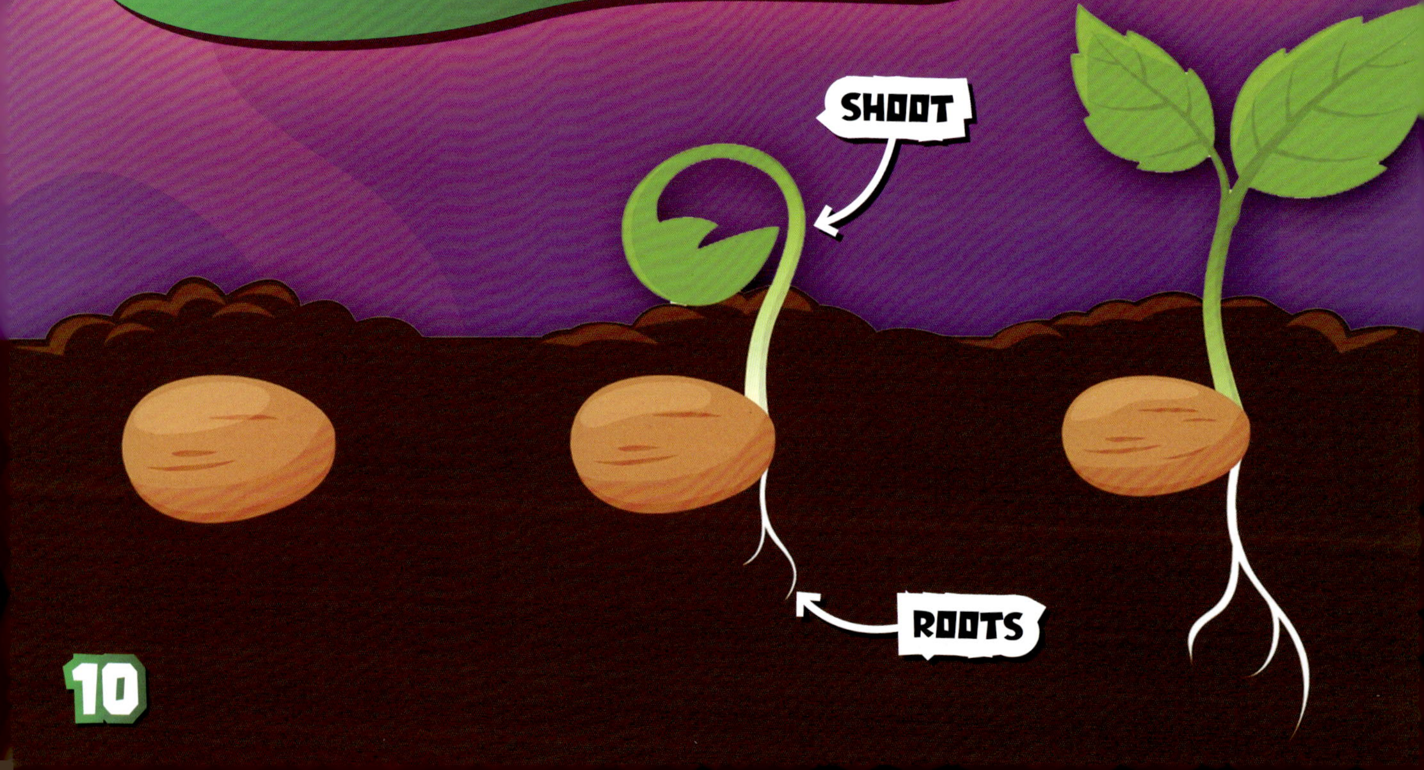

Roots grow deeper into the soil. The plant's shoot pushes up out of the soil. The shoot grows up towards sunlight. The plant then grows leaves as it gets bigger.

PARTS OF A PLANT

The different parts of a plant all have a job to do.

THE ROOTS TAKE IN WATER AND NUTRIENTS FROM THE SOIL. THEY ALSO KEEP THE PLANT STEADY AND IN PLACE.

Super plants have super roots!

THE STEM KEEPS THE PLANT UPRIGHT. WATER AND NUTRIENTS TRAVEL UP THE STEM.

LEAVES TAKE IN SUNLIGHT. PLANTS USE THIS SUNLIGHT TO CREATE THEIR OWN FOOD.

SOME PLANTS HAVE FLOWERS. THIS IS WHERE THE PLANT'S SEEDS ARE MADE.

FLOWERS

Flowers are nature's colorful superstars. Their bright petals <u>attract</u> bees, butterflies, and birds. These visitors carry <u>pollen</u> to other plants. This spreads the pollen and helps to make new seeds.

Flowers come in all kinds of shapes, sizes, colors, and scents. Most flowers only bloom for a short part of the year. Some flowers bloom in cold weather, while other plants bloom in warm weather.

It's a superpower to be able to grow in so many different places!

TREES

Trees are the giants of the plant world. They have powerful trunks that help them stand tall, and their strong branches reach high into the sky.

Lots of animals make their homes inside trees.

Some trees have an amazing superpower—they grow fruit! Fruit contains the seeds that will help more trees spread and grow. Oranges, apples, and pears are all kinds of fruit that grow on trees.

There are two types of trees—deciduous and coniferous.

Deciduous trees lose their leaves in autumn when the weather gets colder. The leaves turn brown and fall off. Deciduous trees grow more leaves once things get warmer in spring.

Coniferous trees have leaves all year round. Their leaves have a waxy covering that helps them stand up against the harsh winter weather.

Both types of trees protect themselves from harsh weather—that's their superpower.

WILD WONDERS

Wild plants grow on their own without anyone planting or watering them. They survive in forests, deserts, mountains, and even rocky cliffs. Their superpowers help them adapt to hot, cold, wet, or dry places.

Some plants grow better in hot, dry places. Other plants grow better in wet and rainy places. Different plants need different things to grow, but all plants need water and light.

SUPER SCIENCE CHALLENGE

Are you ready to become a science superhero? Take this quiz and check your answers on page 23.

1. Trees make their own food using sunlight. (True/False)
2. Flowers attract insects with their bright petals. (True/False)
3. All trees lose their leaves in the winter. (True/False)
4. Wild plants can only grow if people water them. (True/False)
5. Some plants grow food that people and animals can eat. (True/False)

You have completed this Super Science book and have now become a

★ SCIENCE SUPERHERO! ★

Keep exploring, asking questions, and discovering amazing things about the world.

Answers:
1. True. 2. True. 3. False: Coniferous trees have leaves all year round.
4. False: Wild plants grow without people helping them. 5. True.

GLOSSARY

ADAPT	change over time to suit the environment
ATTRACT	to cause someone or something to be drawn towards a thing or person
BLOOM	to grow flowers
GASES	things that are like air, which fill any space available
NUTRIENTS	natural substances that plants and animals need to grow and stay healthy
POLLEN	the yellow powder made by a flowering plant
SCENTS	smells
SURVIVE	to stay alive

INDEX